D1412308

# *WHAT ARE PROTEINS?*

ANNA KINGSTON

**Britannica**
Educational Publishing

IN ASSOCIATION WITH

**ROSEN**
EDUCATIONAL SERVICES

Published in 2019 by Britannica Educational Publishing (a trademark of Encyclopædia Britannica, Inc.) in association with The Rosen Publishing Group, Inc.
29 East 21st Street, New York, NY 10010

Distributed exclusively by Rosen Publishing.
To see additional Britannica Educational Publishing titles, go to rosenpublishing.com.

First Edition

**Britannica Educational Publishing**
J. E. Luebering: Executive Director, Core Editorial
Mary Rose McCudden: Editor, Britannica Student Encyclopedia

**Rosen Publishing**
Kathy Kuhtz Campbell: Senior Editor
Nelson Sá: Art Director
Nicole Russo-Duca: Series Designer/Book Layout
Cindy Reiman: Photography Manager
Nicole DiMella: Photo Researcher

### Library of Congress Cataloging-in-Publication Data

Names: Kingston, Anna, author.
Title: What are proteins? / Anna Kingston.
Description: New York: Britannica Educational Publishing, in Association with Rosen Educational Services, 2019. | Series: Let's find out! Good health | Audience: Grades 1–4. | Includes bibliographical references and index.
Identifiers: LCCN 2017050391| ISBN 9781538302989 (library bound) | ISBN 9781538302996 (pbk.) | ISBN 9781538303009 (6 pack)
Subjects: LCSH: Proteins in human nutrition—Juvenile literature. | Nutrition—Juvenile literature. | Proteins—Juvenile literature.
Classification: LCC QP551 .K4937 2019 | DDC 613.2/82—dc23
LC record available at https://lccn.loc.gov/2017050391

*Manufactured in the United States of America*

**Photo credits**: Cover, back cover, pp, 1, 16, interior pages background Syda Productions/Shutterstock.com; p. 4 SolStock/E+/Getty Images; p. 5 Maskot/Getty Images; p. 6 eveleen/Shutterstock.com; p. 7 Kike Calvo /NATIONAL GEOGRAPHIC IMAGE COLLECTION/Getty Images; p. 8 Encyclopædia Britannica, Inc.; p. 9 Rohit Seth/Shutterstock.com; p. 10 Josef Pittner/Shutterstock.com; p. 11 Designua/Shutterstock.com; p. 12 Kateryna Kon/Shutterstock.com; p. 13 Evan Oto/Science Source; p. 14 joshya/Shutterstock.com; p. 15 Laguna Design/Science Source; p. 17 Jose Luis Pelaez/The Image Bank/Getty Images; p. 18 a_namenko /iStock/Thinkstock; p. 19 petejerkk/Shutterstock.com; p. 20 vitapix/E+/Getty Images; p. 21 Kim_Schott/iStock /Thinkstock; p. 22 Sergey Novikov/Shutterstock.com; p. 23 vchal/Shutterstock.com; p. 24 Issouf Sanogo/AFP /Getty Images; p. 25 BURGER/PHANIE/Canopy/Getty Images; p. 26 Jim Bowie/Shutterstock.com; p. 27 Darryl Brooks/Shutterstock.com; p. 28 Ariel Skelley/DigitalVision/Getty Images; p. 29 Karol Waszkiewicz /Shutterstock.com.

# CONTENTS

# PROTEINS ARE NUTRIENTS

Food can be tasty, but enjoying its flavors is not the main reason that people eat. People eat because they need nutrients! Nutrients are what a body requires to move, grow, and stay alive. All living things need nutrients to function. Plants make some nutrients and take in others from the air and soil. Animals, such as humans, get nutrients from the foods they eat.

Proteins, carbohydrates, fats, minerals,

Protein is one of several nutrients that the human body needs.

Protein keeps your body strong. About one-sixth of the body's total weight is protein.

▶▶

**COMPARE AND CONTRAST**
How is protein like the other kinds of nutrients? How is it different?

vitamins, and water are all nutrients. Proteins are needed for body tissue to grow and repair itself. After water and possibly fat, protein is the most abundant material in the human body.

Carbohydrates supply most of the energy the body needs. Fats store extra energy for the body. Minerals and vitamins keep the body healthy. Water has many uses in the body. It makes up most of the body's weight.

# Amino Acids

The human body has many types of proteins, which it uses in several ways. Proteins are involved in the processes of growth, movement, reproduction, repair, digestion, and aging.

Proteins are made up of groups of molecules called amino acids. A molecule is the smallest unit of a substance that has all the properties of that substance. For instance, a water molecule

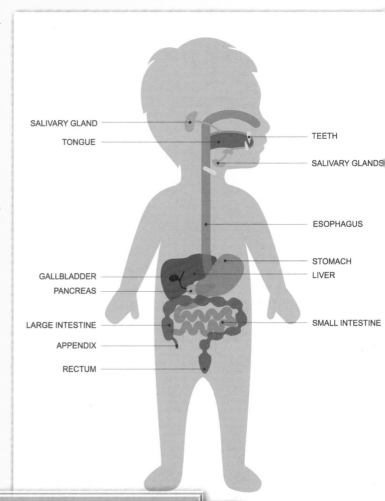

SALIVARY GLAND

TONGUE

TEETH

SALIVARY GLANDS

ESOPHAGUS

STOMACH

LIVER

GALLBLADDER

PANCREAS

SMALL INTESTINE

LARGE INTESTINE

APPENDIX

RECTUM

The digestive system is made up of the parts of the body that break down food into forms that the body can use.

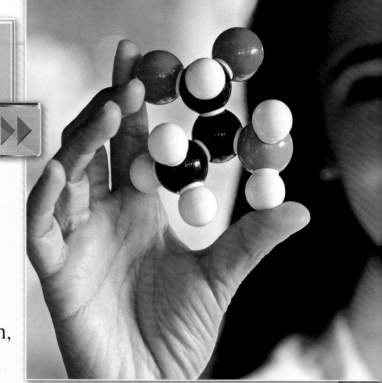

This scientist is holding a model of a molecule of the amino acid alanine.

is the smallest unit that is still water. Molecules are made of even smaller bits called atoms. Amino acid molecules consist of atoms of carbon, hydrogen, oxygen, nitrogen, and sometimes sulfur.

More than 100 kinds of amino acids are found in nature. However, only twenty kinds are the building blocks of all proteins in living things. Amino acids combine in various patterns to make different proteins. Much of the protein-making in the body happens in the liver.

COMPARE AND CONTRAST

How are molecules similar to atoms? How are they different?

7

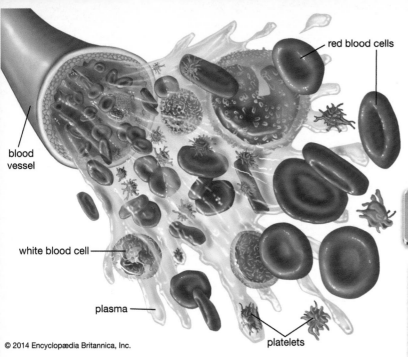

red blood cells

blood vessel

white blood cell

plasma

platelets

© 2014 Encyclopædia Britannica, Inc.

Blood is made up of red blood cells, white blood cells, platelets, and plasma.

Each protein has its own sequence of amino acids. The sequence determines the shape and function of the protein. This means that each protein has a specific mix of amino acids (including many repeating ones) arranged in a specific order.

Most common proteins contain more than 100 amino acids. For example, hemoglobin, a protein found in red blood cells, is made of 287 amino acids.

Plants produce all twenty types of amino acid that they need. The human body, on the other hand, can make only eleven of the twenty required types. People need to get the other nine amino acids from the food they eat. These nine are known as the essential amino acids. They are histidine, isoleucine, leucine, lysine, methionine, phenylalanine, threonine, tryptophan, and valine.

People can get the nine essential amino acids by eating a variety of foods.

# FIBROUS PROTEINS

The two big groups of proteins are fibrous proteins and globular proteins. Fibrous proteins are shaped like fibers, or threads. They are made up of long chains of amino acids that are arranged into strands or sheets.

Fibrous proteins are found in the fur, quills, scales, nails, feathers, horns, antlers, and hooves of animals. They also are a part of skin, including human skin. Fibrous proteins are found in bone, tendons, and cartilage as well. Tendons

Antlers, like those on this elk, have fibrous proteins in them.

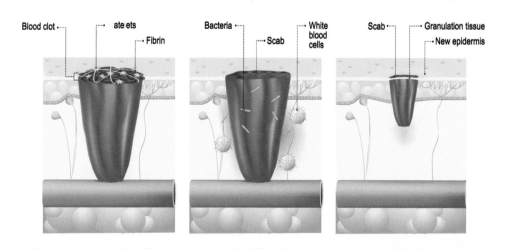

Blood clot ···→ ate ets
···→ Fibrin
Bacteria ···→ ···→ Scab
White blood cells
Scab ···→ ···→ Granulation tissue
···→ New epidermis

Fibrin plays an important role in the clotting process, keeping the body from losing too much blood.

**VOCABULARY**

**Muscles** are the body tissues that animals use for movement.

connect muscles to bones. Cartilage is the rubbery tissue that covers and protects bones at the joints.

Collagen and elastin are fibrous proteins found in the deeper skin layers. Fibrin is a fibrous protein that binds blood platelets together to form blood clots. Clots plug holes that may develop in the walls of blood vessels. This action helps to stop bleeding. Actin and myosin are fibrous proteins that play a big role in helping muscles to move.

# GLOBULAR PROTEINS

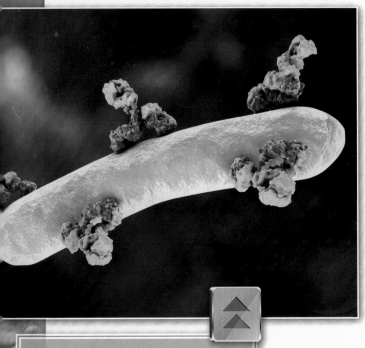

An illustration shows immunoglobulins (bluish purple) attacking a germ (yellow and orange).

While fibrous proteins are shaped like fibers, globular proteins have a globe-like shape. The amino acid chains in globular proteins are folded up into a round structure.

There are many kinds of globular proteins in the human body. Immunoglobulins, or antibodies, are one sort of globular protein. They fight harmful materials, such as germs, that enter the body.

## COMPARE AND CONTRAST

How are enzymes and hormones different? In what ways are they the same?

Most enzymes are globular proteins. Enzymes are catalysts, or substances that control how quickly chemical reactions occur. These reactions are the processes that keep all plants and animals functioning. Enzymes help the body to perform such tasks as digestion and growing new cells.

Some hormones are globular proteins. Hormones tell cells and body parts to do certain things. For example, hormones tell the body when to grow and when to stop growing. The hormones insulin and glucagon maintain safe levels of glucose (a kind of sugar) in the blood.

This is an illustration of trypsin, an enzyme that breaks down proteins into amino acids.

## Oxygen Transport Cycle

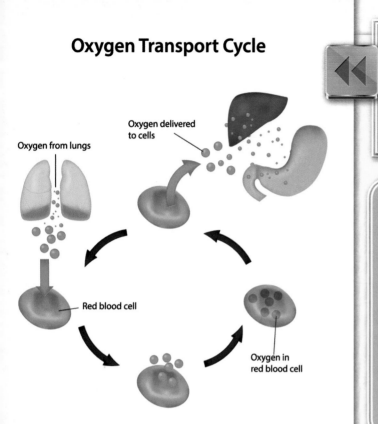

Oxygen from lungs

Oxygen delivered to cells

Red blood cell

Oxygen in red blood cell

The hemoglobin in red blood cells carries oxygen from the lungs throughout the body.

**VOCABULARY**

**Cell membranes** are the thin but tough walls around cells. They let useful substances enter cells. They block the entry of harmful substances.

Transport proteins are globular proteins that carry substances from one place in the body to another. Hemoglobin is a transport protein in red blood cells. It picks up oxygen as it moves through lung tissue and then carries it to the rest of the body. Other transport proteins are found in cell membranes. These proteins shuttle nutrients and waste products from one side of the membrane to the other.

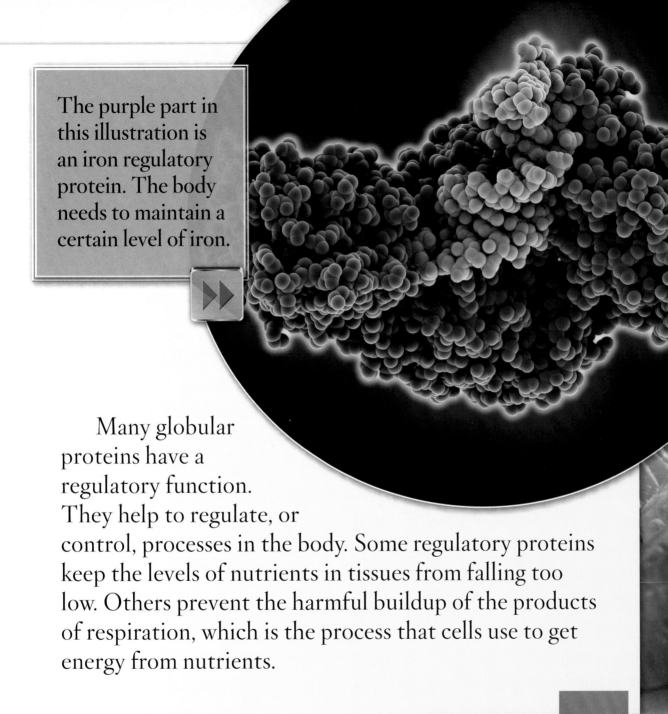

The purple part in this illustration is an iron regulatory protein. The body needs to maintain a certain level of iron.

Many globular proteins have a regulatory function. They help to regulate, or control, processes in the body. Some regulatory proteins keep the levels of nutrients in tissues from falling too low. Others prevent the harmful buildup of the products of respiration, which is the process that cells use to get energy from nutrients.

# SOURCES OF PROTEIN

Foods from animal sources supply people with all the essential amino acids. These foods include meat, poultry, fish, eggs, and dairy products, such as milk, yogurt, and cheese. They are complete proteins.

Some animal sources of protein are less healthy than others. For example, eating lots of processed meats is tied to higher rates of cancer. Bacon, cured ham, corned beef, canned meats, precooked meats, and sausages are processed meats. Processed meats also are linked to diabetes and heart disease.

Eggs, meat, fish, and milk are all animal sources of protein.

Foods from plant sources are incomplete proteins. Plant proteins may lack some of the essential amino acids or have low levels of them. However, people can get all the essential amino acids by eating a mix of different protein-containing plant foods. Good plant sources of protein are nuts, seeds, legumes, and tofu. Legumes include peas, beans, and soybeans. Tofu is a protein-rich food made from soybeans.

## COMPARE AND CONTRAST

How are proteins from plants like those from animals? How are they different?

Plant sources of protein include nuts, legumes, soy milk, and tofu. Broccoli has some protein, too.

Plant sources supply all or much of the protein in the diets of vegetarians, who eat no meat, poultry, or fish. Many nonvegetarians around the world also get protein from plant foods, which are often less expensive and lower in fat than meat.

Some people add extra protein to their regular diet. One popular way to get extra protein is to use protein powder. Protein powder usually

Whey powder is made from whey, a watery product of the cheese-making process.

contains whey, soy, or casein protein. Whey and casein are present in milk, while soy comes from the soybean plant. People often make shakes with protein powder, or they mix it into other foods. Bodybuilders and other athletes use it to build up muscle. Protein powder can be a good source of protein for vegetarians, too.

# How Much Protein Do People Need?

How much protein a person needs to eat depends on many factors, including how old a person is and whether that person is male or female. In 2015, the US Department of Agriculture (USDA) recommended that kids from ages nine to thirteen eat 34 grams (1.2 ounces) of protein each day. It recommended 46 g (1.6 oz.) per day for girls who are ages

No matter what age you are, it is important to get enough protein in your diet.

Like any other egg, a hard-boiled egg provides about 6 grams (0.2 ounce) of protein.

fourteen to eighteen and 52 g (1.8 oz.) for boys of the same age.

A chicken breast has about 30 g (1.0 oz.) of protein, while a can of tuna has 40 g (1.4 oz.). A large egg has 6 g (0.2 oz.) of protein, and a cup of milk has 8 g (0.3 oz.). A serving of tofu has 20 g (0.7 oz.) of protein.

The USDA has a website, ChooseMyPlate.gov, to help people plan healthy diets. It advises eating protein from a mix of sources.

**THINK ABOUT IT**

Why do you think teens need more protein than younger kids?

# THE IMPORTANCE OF PROTEIN

Because protein plays many roles in the body, it is important to consume enough of it. Protein is particularly important for people who are active. In fact, doctors recommend that people eat a protein-rich food, such as yogurt or nuts, after exercise.

After playing a lively game like volleyball, consider eating a protein-rich snack.

The swelling in one of this person's legs is the result of edema.

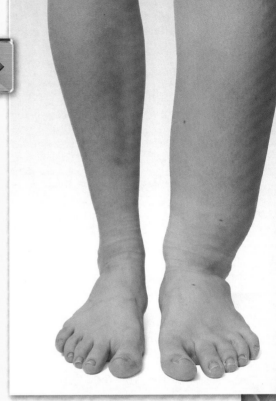

If people do not eat enough protein, or if the proteins that they eat do not provide all the essential amino acids, problems can result. People who do not get enough protein may feel weak and tired. They also may lack muscle tone. Another clue that a person may not be getting enough protein is edema. Edema is a buildup of fluids that occurs most often in the legs and feet. Finally, a lack of protein can cause anemia, or problems with the body's red blood cells. Anemia makes people feel weak and dizzy.

**THINK ABOUT IT**

Do you think you get enough protein?

# MALNUTRITION

Malnutrition is a condition in which a person does not get the right amount of nutrients. The most common form of malnutrition is protein-energy malnutrition. This type of malnutrition occurs when a person gets too little protein, too few calories, or both.

Kwashiorkor is a severe form of protein malnutrition. It is common among young children in developing countries. Children who suffer from kwashiorkor may get enough

This child at a center for displaced people in the Central African Republic shows signs of kwashiorkor.

calories. They eat mostly starchy foods, such as cereal grains and cassava. However, these foods alone do not provide enough protein. Kwashiorkor causes weakness, anemia, failure to grow, and swelling of the belly.

Marasmus is another kind of malnutrition. It results from not taking in enough protein and calories. Children with marasmus do not grow properly, and their fat and muscles waste away. Other symptoms include dehydration and dry, loose skin. Marasmus occurs mostly among very young children, usually during famines.

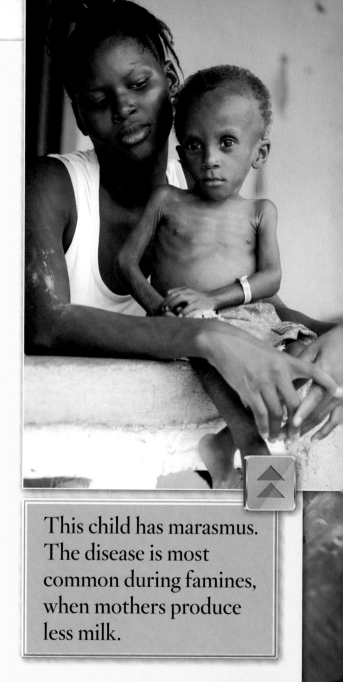

This child has marasmus. The disease is most common during famines, when mothers produce less milk.

# Too Much Protein

Getting too much protein can be a problem. Diets that are very high in protein can damage the kidneys. People who eat too much protein also tend not to get enough of the other nutrients they need. For example, some protein-heavy diets do not provide the carbohydrates that the body requires. This lack of carbohydrates

While meat provides the protein your body requires, there is no need to eat a whole steak by yourself!

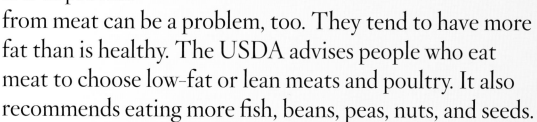

Lean proteins such as fish, whole grains, and lots of vegetables are all part of a healthy diet.

is unhealthy, especially in the long run.

Diets with lots of protein from meat can be a problem, too. They tend to have more fat than is healthy. The USDA advises people who eat meat to choose low-fat or lean meats and poultry. It also recommends eating more fish, beans, peas, nuts, and seeds.

People who try to add extra protein to their diets do not always make healthy choices, either. For example, they may eat protein bars, which are often high in sugar.

## THINK ABOUT IT

Most Americans consume more protein than their bodies need. Why do you think this happens?

# ESSENTIAL AND USEFUL

The word "protein" comes from the Greek word *proteios*, which means "primary" or "first." Proteins are of primary importance to living things, and the body needs them to stay healthy. For that reason, it is necessary for people to include enough protein in their diets. The proteins in foods provide the amino acids that the body uses to make all the proteins it requires.

Some scientists study the proteins that the body makes. The exact number of protein types in the body is not known. So far, scientists have discovered many thousands.

When you go shopping with your parents, look for healthy protein sources such as milk.

Proteins make spider silk stretchy and strong. Some spiders spin silks that are stronger than steel piano wire.

Although proteins are essential to human health, they are useful to people for other reasons. Many commercial products contain proteins. For example, laundry detergents often contain the proteins called enzymes. The enzymes help to clean clothing by breaking down the proteins in stains. Proteins also may be found in some plastics.

Many useful proteins are found in nature. Manufacturers can get proteins from milk, spider webs, mushrooms, and other natural sources. Other useful proteins are made by scientists in labs.

**THINK ABOUT IT**

If you were a scientist, what would you want to learn about proteins?

# Glossary

**abundant** Existing in large numbers.

**amino acid** One of the building blocks from which proteins are made.

**blood vessels** A system of tubes that carry blood throughout the body.

**cancer** A disease that causes certain cells in the body to grow out of control.

**carbohydrates** Nutrients, such as starches and sugars, that give the body the energy it needs.

**cell** The smallest unit with the basic properties of life.

**chemical reaction** The changing of matter into new types of matter.

**dehydration** The loss of water or other body fluids.

**diabetes** A disease caused by too much of a sugar called glucose in the body.

**digestion** The breaking down of food into a form that the body can use.

**essential** Totally necessary.

**famine** An extreme shortage of food in an area.

**joint** A place, such as the elbow, where the body can bend.

**kidneys** Body parts that create urine from waste that they remove from the blood.

**lab** A place where scientists work and do experiments.

**legume** One of several plants in the pea family, such as beans, peas, peanuts, and soybeans.

**nutrient** One of the things in food that the body needs to function and maintain itself.

**platelet** A small, round, thin blood cell that helps blood to stop flowing from a cut by forming thick and sticky clots.

**tissue** A group of cells that work together to do a specific job.

# FOR MORE INFORMATION

## Books

Black, Vanessa. *Protein Foods.* Minneapolis, MN: Jump!, Inc., 2017.

Bodden, Valerie. *Proteins* (Healthy Plates). Mankato, MN: Creative Education, 2015.

Boothroyd, Jennifer. *What's on My Plate? Choosing from the Five Food Groups.* Minneapolis, MN: Lerner Publications, 2016.

Canavan, Thomas. *Fueling the Body: Digestion and Nutrition* (How Your Body Works). New York, NY: PowerKids Press, 2016.

Centore, Michael. *Protein* (Know Your Food). Broomall, PA: Mason Crest, 2018.

Randolph, Joanne. *Taste and Digestion* (Amazing Human Body). New York, NY: Enslow Publishing, 2018.

Ventura, Marne. *Nutrition Myths, Busted!* (Science Myths, Busted). North Mankato, MN: 12-Story Library, 2017.

## Websites

**Arizona State University School of Life Sciences**
https://askabiologist.asu.edu/venom/what-are-proteins
Facebook: @Dr.Biology; Instagram: @askabiologist; Twitter: @Drbiology

**National Institutes of Health (NIH)**
https://ghr.nlm.nih.gov/primer/howgeneswork/protein
Facebook: @nih.gov; Twitter: @NIH

**Sciencing**
https://sciencing.com/characteristics-protein-8460468.html
Facebook and Twitter: @RealSciencing

# INDEX